# NO FLUFF SERIES

**LEARN ABOUT A TOPIC
IN UNDER 30 PAGES**

# HOW TO MAXIMIZE PARDOT CAPABILITIES AND ACHIEVE OPTIMAL MARKETING REPORTING WITH SALESFORCE SALES CLOUD

**NO FLUFF PRESS**
PRINTED IN THE UNITED STATES OF AMERICA

How to Maximize Pardot Capabilities and Achieve
Optimal Marketing Reporting with Salesforce Sales Cloud

ISBN-13: 978-1-955559-02-7
ISBN-10: 1-955559-02-3

Printed in the United States of America

First Printing, 2021

No Fluff Press
U.S.A.
www.nofluffseries.com

# Introduction

SALESFORCE SALES CLOUD IS A POWERFUL CRM tool with a number of capabilities that can be customized and configured to your company's business processes. Except now, you and your company are looking to take your CRM to the next level, by enhancing your marketing specific initiatives in order to centralize everything in a single platform. This allows you to optimize campaign execution, monitor ongoing campaign metrics and be able to report on final campaign performance. It is every marketer's dream to be able to exemplify what they are contributing to the company's bottom line by assisting the sales department in generating leads with actual data driven reports that corroborate marketing efforts. Ask any salesperson and they would tell you that they desire to have quality leads delivered to progress the sales cycle in the most efficient manner possible. And it is every other department's goal to see this in a fluid manner for the company to continuously grow and prosper. Not just because of increased bottom line, but because of the ability to make data driven decisions from reports.

In this book, we will tackle the pertinent features of Pardot that are specific to marketing initiatives and their campaign impacts (or lack thereof) to know what to invest more marketing dollars in and what marketing activities to divest out of. The marketing department has nearly the largest budget allocated within an organization, and it is critical that these funds are utilized to drive results. Numerous marketing books are cumbersome and complicate this process and by the end of those books, you really do not know where to start. These other books act like 'Marketing' is an exact science, but in reality, it is truly trial and error and with experience, allows you to become more strategic in your processes. This book breaks down key features in Pardot that can result in you being able to obtain reporting metrics that can demonstrate the effectiveness of marketing initiatives.

# Step 1: Understanding Pardot Terminology

THIS SECTION IS RELATIVELY SHORT, but do not underestimate its importance, as these terms will be used throughout this book. It is critical that you understand what is being referenced when reading each step.

## GENERAL TERMS

- **Edition of Pardot:** This is the version of Pardot your company purchased. Examples of editions include Growth, Plus, Advanced or Premium Edition. Each edition has varying capabilities in the order the editions were written. Therefore, it is important to know which edition of Pardot you are using, as some of the capabilities discussed in this book may not be available or are limited within the edition your company has purchased.
- **Lightning or Classic:** These two words will come up depending on if you are working for a company that has had Salesforce for a while. Lightning is the newest Salesforce User Interface (a.k.a. "look and feel") of Salesforce itself. Classic is the older Salesforce User Interface. If your company recently purchased Salesforce, then you will be automatically defaulted to Lightning. If your company has had Salesforce for a while, then they still may be using Classic and may eventually need to migrate (switch over) to Lightning.
- **Business to Business (B-to-B) and/or Business to Consumer (B-to-C) Selling:** Salesforce out-of-the-box is defaulted for businesses that sell 'business to business' with the use of contact records associated to account records. If you are a company that sells only 'business to consumer', or needs the ability to sell both 'business to business' and 'business to consumer'; then this feature is called "Person Accounts" ('business to consumer' selling within Salesforce) and you can request this feature to be enabled.

## PARDOT EVERYDAY USER TERMS

- **Prospects:** Do not assume you know what this means because in Pardot, every individual that is able to be part of a Campaign is a Prospect. Even if the individual (person or entity) is already a customer and has used your products/services prior, this individual will still be designated as a Prospect.

This is because individuals within Pardot can still be part of a Campaign and are classified as Prospects regardless of their purchase history. Of course, there will be field designations and Opportunity history to designate 'Customers' versus 'Prospects', but that is based on your custom classifications and/or fields within Pardot and your Salesforce CRM.

- **Assets:** These are the items that are being created or have been used within an actual Campaign. Examples include, the targeted segment of prospects called lists (specific criteria that includes only certain prospects), forms, landing pages and emails that can all be used within a Campaign. This 'Asset' term will be used constantly, as these are the items you pull reports on and are used to help determine the performance of each Campaign executed within Pardot.

- **Engagement Studio:** This is a feature for when you are building a Campaign that has defined logic and follows a step-by-step process with the use of multiple emails that are sent at specified time periods. In essence, this is like your 'Campaign Canvas' that allows you to drag and drop steps that provides a detailed visual to ensure the Campaign is built to your business requirements to obtain optimal results.

- **List Emails:** Are emails created for only a one time or single use send. Think of List Emails as another form of email blasts, but tracked via Pardot tracking capabilities. Just know these types of emails cannot be utilized as Templates nor can be utilized within the Engagement Studio.

- **Email Templates:** Are emails created for automated purposes with the use of the Engagement Studio functionality, for Autoresponder emails and for Sales to send 'one-to-one' email sends.

- **Fields:** This must be specified to distinguish the fields that are created and used within Salesforce CRM, versus the fields that are created within Pardot. Fields will exist in both systems, and some will be the exact same between the two systems for integration and field mapping purposes. Other fields will differ between both systems as they may be used for specific purposes.

- **Related Lists:** This is a list of records for each specific Object(s) that are associated to the record you are viewing. For example, let's say you are on a specific Account record called "Testing Center 123", then a related list to this Account could be the Contact Object with the actual contact records that work at that Account. Simply put, Related Lists display information by Object and lists the specific records within those Objects, for easy reference of related items to the actual record you are viewing.

- **Page Layouts:** This is where fields are positioned on the page within

Salesforce Sales Cloud. You are able to create designated sections for users to easily reference fields that are applicable to that section. You can also determine which related Objects (a.k.a. 'Related Lists') that are shown on each Page Layout to display related information. Lastly, you are able to add components or Visualforce components onto the Page. With the use of Pardot, there are Visualforce components that are recommended to be added onto the Lead/Contact Page Layout within Salesforce Sales Cloud.

- **Record Types:** Allows you to control only relevant information displayed per the Record Type. For example, on the Account Object, a company may want to create Record Types for their 'retail' accounts and their 'wholesale' accounts. This way, you'll have the chance to choose which fields and related lists are displayed for the retail accounts, which may differ from the fields and related lists you want displayed on the wholesale accounts.
- **Buttons:** Can be standard or custom built, and examples of buttons include "Edit", "Clone", "Delete", etc. These are items users click on that then allow them to do something and/or can run an automation. There are Pardot specific buttons that are recommended to be added to the Page Layout of Leads/ Contacts Object.

## LEVEL OF ACCESS TERMS

- **Salesforce Users:** These are the people that have or had access to your Salesforce CRM. Users are the personnel that will be working within your Salesforce and/or Pardot, depending on the license type that is assigned per User.
- **Pardot Users:** Users that have some sort of access to Pardot at varying levels based on their assigned Pardot Role.
- **Salesforce Profiles:** Typically created for each department (or by department subsets) and assigned to each user that permits the relevant security access to items within your Salesforce. There are a few layers of security and level of access that can be permitted to users. Just know, Profiles are required to be assigned to each user and can be a great starting point to get an idea of which users have access to various items within your Salesforce.
- **Salesforce Roles:** This reflects the hierarchy of users within your Company. It is important that this is set up correctly, as Roles have an effect on the potential access of other Role records, for team reporting and other items.
- **Pardot Roles:** This feature is similar to 'Salesforce Profiles', as this grants a user the appropriate level of access to Pardot specific items. Understand, that 'Pardot Roles' are aligned with 'Salesforce Profiles' and not 'Salesforce Roles'. 'Pardot Roles' is the level of access that is permitted per user within Pardot.

# Step 2: Pardot AppExchange Install & Setup

FIRST OFF, CONGRATULATIONS ON PURCHASING Pardot and entering into the world of marketing automation. With any newly purchased software, most personnel think that they will now just login to Salesforce (or any system for that matter) and that Pardot (or the newly purchased system) will just appear and automatically connect itself to other systems used throughout the company, which is not the case. An admin or a user with the appropriate permissions will need to install the Pardot Package from the Salesforce AppExchange and go through the install process. This will then permit you to have the Pardot components installed within your Salesforce.

Second, have your Salesforce admin (or a user with the appropriate level of access) click on 'Marketing Setup' to enable Pardot within your Salesforce, and also assign a user whom will be the admin of Pardot, for them to be able to gain access to Pardot.

These two items discussed above are one of the biggest struggles for clients that have just purchased Pardot. These steps are required in order for you or your admin, to have access to Pardot components and also have the ability to login initially to start the implementation of Pardot.

**Helpful Hint:** The Salesforce/Pardot connector that integrates both Salesforce and Pardot will be set to "Paused" initially after the above two items are complete. This is okay, as you can setup Pardot specific items while the sync of data between the two systems is paused. It is recommended to have the majority of Pardot features implemented, prior to activating the sync.

# Step 3: Website Tracking & Domain Management

WEBSITE TRACKING AND DOMAIN MANAGEMENT are core features of Pardot and are broken out in their own sections for you to clearly understand the steps involved with each of these features. These features may require you to include your IT Team and/or Web Developer to implement these capabilities.

**Website Tracking:**
The initial admin user now has access to Pardot and the first item that is ideal to get up and running is your organization's website tracking. You can simply create a Campaign record within Pardot by clicking on the **Pardot tab** > **Marketing** > **Campaigns** or utilize the Pardot Lightning B2B Marketing App. Click on 'New' to create a new Campaign record and name the Campaign something like 'Website Tracking' and then click save. From this newly created record screen, located on the top right, click on the button called 'View Tracking Code'. This generates a tracking code for you to provide to your organization's web developer, to be added onto the company website. This code has the specific IDs to pass through the tracked website activity directly into your Pardot instance.

Once the code is added onto your company's website, you will need to update the Tracking Opt-In Preferences to be in compliance with varying countries to alert website visitors via a pop up to Opt-In. Setting the Tracking Opt-In Preferences is located under the Pardot 'Admin' tab and then selecting the option called 'Domain Management'. On the top right hand side, there is a button called 'Edit Tracking Opt-In Preferences' and a screen will appear with the message you would like to create for your website visitors regarding being tracked, the style of the look and feel of the pop up/messaging and the link styles. Depending on who you are marketing to and where you are located in the world, you have the option to select to request opt-in confirmations for all visitors or you can specify which countries you require opt-in confirmations for varying visitors. You and your company may need to consult with legal counsel to determine exceptions (if applicable), as laws can vary and change. Keep in mind that your organization must keep up-to-date with these website activity tracking laws at all times.

## Domain Management:

There are two parts to the Domain Management feature.

1. **Email Sending Domains** – this is where your company's domain(s) are inputted for marketing users to send out mass e-mails with email addresses that have the company domain configured. Your internal IT personnel will need to update the SPF and DomainKey policies to include Pardot values for verification purposes. Pardot provides the 'Expected Entry' per required item to make it easier for your internal IT team to know what needs to be added under each required item that needs to be verified within Pardot to work accordingly. Pardot will let you know within the Email Sending Domain section the status of each item that needs to be verified and which ones that have not. All items need to be set to 'Verified' by Pardot in order for you to start using the 'Email Sending Domain' accordingly. In simple terms, once verified, the email sending domain is the 'From' email address domain that can be included when utilizing marketing automation and sending out emails to your customers/prospects.

2. **Tracker Domains** – this is the URL domain(s) that will be used to create landing page links within Pardot. One of the most common tracker domains created is something like this: hello.companydomain.com. This tracker domain will be the prefix (or the start) of every URL link of any custom landing page developed that will have a "/customlandingpagenamehere" added at the end of the tracker domain each time a new landing page is created. All this does is generate a unique link per page, as this is required. A full example of a landing page using the tracker domain is as follows: hello.companydomain.com/contactus. This example is the Contact Us landing page on your website using the Tracker Domain that you just created. You can simply add a Tracking Domain in Pardot by clicking on the button called " + Add Tracker Domain" and add the prefix URL you would like to have that will be used for each landing page created. Internal IT personnel will need to update the DNS to add a CNAME to point to the newly created Tracker Domain to be verified for Pardot purposes. Pardot will need to show the Tracker Domain is 'Validated' and 'Enabled' prior to being able to be utilized when creating landing pages. It is recommended that you set your custom Tracker Domain as the 'Primary' Tracker Domain as well, by clicking on the gear icon at the end of the Tracker Domain record and choosing the option called 'Set as Primary' of the most commonly utilized Tracker Domain that you and team will use most often.

# Step 4: Pardot Fields

PARDOT FIELDS ARE SIMILAR TO fields within your Salesforce CRM. Some of the standard fields within Salesforce CRM already exist within Pardot, while the custom fields that have been added into Salesforce may also need to be added into Pardot. You can add custom fields into Pardot on the following items under the 'Configure Fields' menu option:

**Prospect Fields:** These are fields that can be added into Pardot that are specific to the Lead and Contact Object. Any custom fields that have been added to the Lead and Contact Object that are applicable to marketing initiatives and for segmentation purposes, should be added into Pardot as custom fields. Regardless if a Contact is already a customer or not, Pardot still considers the Contact as a 'Prospect', but other custom fields or standard fields that have been updated to identify the Contact as a 'Customer' will be used within segmentation and Salesforce/Pardot Sync purposes. 'Prospect' fields have 'Sync Behavior' between Salesforce and Pardot, meaning there are options to determine which information (in either Salesforce or Pardot) takes precedence and overwrites one another as the source of truth. This is set on a per field basis and it is important to determine which system or records recently updated, will have the most accurate information possible.

**Account Fields:** These are fields that can be added into Pardot that are specific to the Account Object. It is important to remember that marketing automation markets to people and therefore, custom fields added under 'Account Fields' do not have Sync Behavior settings, as it will only sync information from Salesforce CRM. Account fields are utilized for segmentation and for automation purposes. You will still need to field map which Salesforce fields will be syncing with the custom Account fields that are created within Pardot.

**Helpful Hint:** If you have 'Person Accounts' enabled, then it is highly recommended to add fields that you would like to have 'Sync Behavior' settings applicable for various fields on the Contact Object, instead of the Account Object. This will allow fields that are 'Person Account' specific that were added as custom fields onto the Contact Object, to be utilized on Forms and have 'Sync Behavior' settings designated per field.

**Opportunity Fields:** These are fields that can be added into Pardot that are specific to the Opportunity Object. Similar to Account Fields, custom fields added under 'Opportunity Fields' do not have 'Sync Behavior' settings, as it will only sync information from Salesforce CRM. Opportunity fields are utilized for segmentation and for automation purposes. You will still need to field map which Salesforce fields will be syncing with the custom Opportunity fields that are created within Pardot.

**Custom Objects:** Custom Objects can be synced into Pardot depending on the edition of Pardot you have, though you may need to upgrade to a higher edition of Pardot in order to have this capability. When syncing custom objects, you are simply pulling information from Salesforce CRM into Pardot for segmentation and automation purposes. Instead of the need to field map each field into Pardot for custom objects, you will decide which fields will be displayed within the custom object table in Pardot, as it will only pull this field level detail from Salesforce.

**Helpful Hint:** Be sure the custom object you would like to sync with Pardot is actually related to the Lead or Contact Object, or it will not be useful for marketing automation purposes.

# Step 5: Lead Scoring & Profile Scoring

THERE ARE TWO SEPARATE SCORING methodologies in Pardot: 'Lead Scoring' (a numerical score) and 'Profile Scoring' (a letter grade).

**Lead Scoring:**
Lead Scoring is based on the prospect's interaction with marketing initiatives and sales processes that calculates a numerical value. For example, opening a marketing email, clicking on a link within an email, filling out a form, visiting the company's website and many other items that are all tallied together to determine a numerical Lead Score value. There are items that can reduce a Lead Score, such as having an opportunity that is set to the Closed Lost stage (meaning the Sales Representative lost the deal), which can subtract and reduce the overall Lead Score of a specific 'Prospect' record within Pardot. The 'Prospect' will have all the tracked interactions itemized within their profile and the total Lead Score of the 'Prospect' is added together, based on the interactions that have taken place. In essence, various actions can add to the Lead Score or subtract from the Lead Score, to then determine an ever changing number that helps marketers choose which Prospects are ready to be passed along to sales personnel to be further prospected due to their level of interest in the company's products/services. Those that have not met a specific score or threshold will need to continue to be 'Nurtured' until a high enough score has been met and/or an action has taken place that is of high priority, to then pass along the 'Prospect' to sales personnel. Within Pardot, there are set Scoring Rule Categories that are all on a single page for you to review. Each of these categories is assigned a value that you can update for 'Prospects' to be scored accordingly. Other items that can affect Lead Scoring outside of the standard Scoring Rules are the following:

- Completion Actions
- Page Actions
- Automation Rules
- All of these items will be discussed later in this book, but keep in mind that you can utilize these features to make Lead Scoring adjustments when necessary.

Please note that multiple Lead Scoring methodologies can be implemented depending on the edition of Pardot your company has purchased, which allows varying Lead Scoring models. Multiple Lead Scoring models may be necessary for companies that have different products/services that are sold in other departments that differ based on the score per category that may be more/less valuable per Lead Scoring model. Regardless of how many Lead Scoring methodologies you choose to implement or have available, it is important to test the scoring. Start by testing a typical Prospect's average amount of activities, to ensure scoring is working accordingly and are not getting astronomically high scores that have no actionable meaning, but not too low of scores where no prospect is hitting specific thresholds to trigger a follow up. This will take a good amount of discussions and testing to get a scoring methodology that is aligned with both marketing and sales that represents if a Prospect is 'sales-ready' and alternatively, those that need to have marketing continue to try and increase their Prospect engagement.

**Profile Scoring:**
Profile Scoring is less well known in the marketing automation world, but can be valuable to identify specific individuals that are best to pitch your company's products/services. A Profile Score provides a letter grade instead of a numerical value, and ranges exactly like it did in grade school, from 'F' being the worst and 'A+' for being the best. Profile Scoring is based on fields that provide a 'Grade Adjustment' per field designation. For example, Industry, Department, Title and Company Size are fields that can be designated and be assigned a Profile Score letter grade adjustment, to determine the 'level of fit' of the ideal person at a company or individual whom your company prefers to target and speak with further about your product/service offerings. There can be a number of different 'Profile Scoring' methodologies implemented, and which Profile Score that is assigned is based on how these designated fields of your choosing are populated. Based on the information populated, this can then trigger an 'Automation Rule' (which will be discussed in Step 8 of this book) that designates which 'Profile Scoring' model runs and assigns a letter grade adjustment per category for that specific Profile Score model.

**Helpful Hint:** Just because a Prospect is assigned an 'A' letter grade, does not have any effect on the actual 'Lead Score' of the Prospect. For example, the Profile Score of a Prospect may be an 'A', but their Lead Score may be a score of 10. How to interpret this, is that this may be the ideal person of whom you would like to speak with, but they are not interested in any of the marketing material sent to them, nor are they receptive to any sales touchpoints thus far.

Therefore, this Prospect still needs to be nurtured until the Prospect has a higher engagement to want to learn more about your company's product/service offerings. Even though these two features provided a score of some kind, they still have zero influence over each other. It is important to set the precedence of this with your team as you implement Lead Scoring and Profile Scoring.

# Step 6: Subscription Management

SUBSCRIPTION MANAGEMENT IS WHERE PROSPECTS are able to select from a list of the types of content they wish to receive. This way, Prospects are able to subscribe to specific types of lists, since that is the content they have the most interest in receiving on a recurring basis. Examples include, monthly newsletters, product updates, promotions, company updates and many other categories that your Prospects can choose from to decide which types of information are best for them to want to read or learn more about.

Before sending out emails to Prospects within Pardot, it is important that you set up a Subscription Management selection for Prospects to choose the type of content they would like to receive. If this feature is not configured prior to emailing Prospects, then the only option for these Prospects to not receive emails is to 'Globally Opt-Out' of all marketing communications. Taking this shortcut would be the opposite of the objective regarding the use of marketing automation, so it is vital that Subscription Management is setup prior to emailing prospects.

**Helpful Hint:** Be sure the categories displayed to Prospects are short, yet descriptive and relevant to your type of business. It is not ideal to have general topics or a large number of categories to choose from, as this could confuse Prospects and they may simply choose to just 'Globally Opt-Out' instead. There is a 'Resubscribe' feature within Pardot, which is great to allow 'Prospects' to resubscribe when needed and 'Opt-In' back again at their leisure. But it is ideal to start off the right way by having Subscription Management implemented initially.

# Step 7: Asset Build

ASSETS ARE ITEMS THAT ARE specifically built for Campaigns to track marketing initiatives and to obtain information about each Prospect. You may build these Assets utilizing a drag-and-drop wizard and/or utilize custom HTML/CSS to ensure the look and feel of each Asset follows your company brand. The flexibility is there, and it will come down to the internal resources you have at your disposal or the ability to hire a third party to build Asset templates. Once templates are built per Asset, you can quickly clone the template and update the content and/or picture(s) to save them as actual Assets that will be utilized in a Campaign. If you are cloning off templates, then Campaign builds should be quite simplistic and will come down to the new content per Asset needed, the criteria for the segmented targeted list, updated Completion Actions/Automations and the strategic campaign journey paths created.

Assets within Pardot are the following items:

**Forms:** Are utilized on various Landing Pages that Prospects are able to input their information to request to be contacted, download a whitepaper, gain access to various content, etc. Forms are the gatekeeper to obtaining information about Prospects. As simple as a Form can be, it actually has some of the most capabilities out of any Asset that can be built within Pardot.

For example, when adding fields to a Form that you would like to have Prospects complete, you will have the option to require a field on a per field basis. The field label that is displayed to the Prospect can be changed (rather than keep the internal field name) and you can choose to always display the field regardless if it is already populated within Pardot, to not prefill based on information that is already stored within Pardot, update picklist values to only applicable values to be displayed for that particular Form, determine if a field will be used for 'Progressive Profiling' and lastly if the field is dependent on another field. All of this and more, simply when you are adding a field to a Form, are items that need to be determined on a per field basis. These settings assist with capturing the right information and to have higher form conversion rates, especially with the use of 'Progressive Profiling'. 'Progressive Profiling' is when a Form only displays certain fields (limits which fields to display out of all the fields that are included on the Form) to the Prospect when they are completing the Form itself. So maybe first name, last name and email are the fields that will appear for the Prospect to complete initially. Then the next time the Prospect requests information, maybe the company and phone number are the fields that are only displayed for them to complete and so forth. This way you achieve a much higher form conversion rate and are building out their Prospect profile within Pardot, by capturing information progressively over a period of time.

Another item within the Form asset that you will most likely utilize constantly for nearly every Form (if not every Form) is Completion Actions. A Form is one area you can designate these types of actions, that usually run after a prospect successfully submits a Form. There are several options to choose from in a drop down menu of what you would like to happen to this Prospect after this specific Form is submitted with the use of Completion Actions. Examples include: add them to a list, adjust their Lead Score, add as a member of a Campaign and designate their Campaign Status (like responded or sent status), change a field value, add a tag, create a Task for an internal User to contact the Prospect and many other items. In essence, Completion Actions determine what can happen next to the Prospect. Each Completion Action is clearly labeled per option that is available and is very simple to know what happens to the Prospect by creating new or reviewing existing Completion Actions per Form.

**Helpful Hint:** Most likely you will have multiple Completion Actions per Form and it is critical that all the necessary Completion Actions are created per Form to achieve optimal reporting. The whole point of this book is to accomplish Closed Loop Reporting, starting with marketing initiatives and how these efforts have assisted sales and the impact of these efforts to the company bottom line. One of the main ways to accomplish this is through Completion Actions and clearly defining each action, so records are associated to each other and followed up with accordingly for optimal reporting purposes.

Now that you know what a Form asset is and nearly all of its features, let's move on to Landing Pages in order to have these Forms be displayed within an actual page for Prospects to visit and complete.

*How do these work within another website? Natpur?*

**Landing Pages:** A page where a Prospect visits (maybe a tab on your webpage) or was re-directed to (either from an email received or an ad the Prospect clicked on) where there is content and usually a Form for the Prospect to complete. Landing Pages are straight forward within Pardot as the main items you set is the name of the page URL, choose which Form you created that should be on the Landing Page, choose the content layout template (out of the box templates can be used and/or you can create your own templates positioning where content, pictures and forms are positioned) and then add the content you wish to include, on a per Landing Page basis.

You are able to conduct 'Multivariate Tests' within Pardot, which is just a big word that means to create multiple Landing Pages that have different designs to see which Landing Page performs superior to the other. For example, maybe one Landing Page has no pictures, minimal content and a Form, while the other Landing Page has pictures, a lot of content and a Form. You are able to provide a percentage weight (typically 50/50) to the two Landing Pages, so each Prospect is shown a varying page to determine which Landing Page performed the best. Of course, the Prospect has cookies and if the Prospect clicks the same re-direct link that took the Prospect to the Landing Page originally, they are shown the same page as prior for consistency purposes. There are specific Pardot reports for Multivariate Statistics for you to determine and review which page design performed the best, to utilize as a future reference when building Landing Pages for other Campaigns.

Now you know to utilize a Landing Page to display content, to then capture information about the Prospect with the use of a Form. Prospects need to be directed to these Landing Pages, and one of the most common ways to accomplish this is through Emails that are sent with the use of Pardot marketing automation.

**Emails:** Are the actual emails that will be built and utilized in marketing campaigns that are sent to Prospects. Some emails are more for communicative purposes only (where there are no 'call to actions' for the Prospect to click on that re-directs them to a Landing Page), while most emails will have a 'call to action' to re-direct the Prospect to a Landing Page to complete a Form. Regardless of what the purpose of the email is, please note that there are two types of Emails that can be created within Pardot.

1. **List Emails** – is simple to remember as this feature is utilized for one-time sends only. Think of these emails as bulk email blasts. These can be used to provide various updates, newsletters, notices and anything else

that is needed for a one-time send. Please note, List Emails are not able to be utilized in any automated email campaigns.

2. **Email Templates** – is also simple to remember as this feature is utilized for automated email campaigns that have built out logic, based on specific actions or inactions that have or have not taken place per Prospect. Email Templates can be used as part of a Campaign within the Engagement Studio to build out your 'Campaign Canvas' that displays each step that takes place within the Campaign and determines when Prospects receive emails that were built for the Campaign. Email Templates can also be used as an autoresponder email. Examples of an autoresponder email include a short email that is sent to a Prospect after someone registers for an event to provide a registration confirmation or that the Prospect will be contacted shortly after a Form submission. Lastly, these types of emails can be used for 'one to one' emails for the sales department (or any other department) to utilize the Pardot built email, which can be sent on an individual basis directly from within Salesforce CRM to the Prospect.

Other key Email Asset features include the following:

- **A/B Testing:** A feature that is utilized to determine which subject line of an email provides a greater 'Open' rate. This is a point and click feature that allows you to provide a weighted percentage to subject line A and to subject line B, that will be received by a number of Prospects. Pardot will keep track of which subject line performed the best for you to establish internal best practices regarding email subject line tactics for future Campaigns that are ideal to achieve optimal results.

- **Dynamic Content:** A feature that allows you to create an Email asset for various types of Prospects that tailors to and displays differing content of the email based on criteria that you set. For example, if you are sending an email to a Prospect that has a department classified as finance, then the content of the email can display the favorable terms your company provides regarding invoicing. Compared to a Prospect that is part of the same campaign, but has a department classified as sales, may display content of how your products/services assist sales personnel in surpassing their sales goals. It is the same Email asset they receive, but the content is dynamic, based on set criteria to display specific information relevant to the recipient.

**Segmentation:** The list of Prospects that you would like to include within a Campaign based on a set of rules with criteria to segment only those individuals. Pardot has multiple options when creating a segmentation to allow marketers the flexibility to decide who they would like to target per Campaign.

- **Lists** – These are lists that you can create rules which have specified criteria, that will show you the number of Prospects that match the inputted criteria once you run the rule(s) that were created. If everything looks good, you can associate the matching Prospects to a newly created List and can be used within an email Campaign. All criteria created is by point and click options, so it is simple for marketers to structure these rules and define the target audience per Campaign without the use of any code.

  **Helpful Hint:** Lists are based on criteria that runs each time you have the system look into your Pardot Prospect database to find individuals that match the criteria that was inputted. Therefore, this is not updated afterwards and is utilized as a one-time targeted list.

- **List Options** – With Lists, there are additional options that you are able to set on a per List basis. These options include the following:

  ▶ **Public** – This is the setting to create your 'Subscription Management' lists you would like to display publicly per topic/categories. It is forward facing to your Prospects to choose to opt-in or opt-out of specific communications by topic/categories. Only mark this setting on Lists that you want to include within your Subscription Management options.

  ▶ **CRM Visible** – This is the setting that allows users within Salesforce CRM to manually subscribe a Lead/Contact to a specific List on behalf of the Lead/Contact. This feature comes in handy when sales personnel or customer service departments are communicating with a prospect or client and can suggest or request that they be subscribed to various types of communications. This is a great way for departments to collaborate to ensure a prospect or client can receive the type of content that is of interest to them and subscribe them to various Lists accordingly. Your admin will need to update the Lead/Contact Page Layouts within Salesforce CRM and add the Pardot VisualForce Components to the user assigned Page Layouts, so that everyday Salesforce Users have the ability to subscribe prospects/customers to these lists.

  ▶ **Dynamic Lists** – These are lists that you create rules that have specified criteria that target an audience, but constantly runs and updates on its own to continuously include Prospects that fulfill the specific criteria at any time (hence the word 'dynamic' in the name of this feature). These types of Lists are typically used for marketing campaigns that are considered 'Drip', 'Nurture' and/or other Campaigns that are constantly running in the background and automatically pull prospects that fulfill the dynamic list criteria. All the criteria is created by point and click options, so it is simple for marketers to create these rules and define the target audience per Dynamic List without any code needed.

► **Test** – This is the option to have a designated Test list(s) to utilize when sending email previews, to ensure all is working accordingly. The reason why this is an option, is to ensure the email analytics reporting is not affected by the testing of opens, clicks, etc. These metrics are only counted when the list is not set as a Test list.

# Step 8: Page Actions, Automation Rules & Engagement Studio

PAGE ACTIONS, AUTOMATION RULES, AND Engagement Studio are specific features to add automation within Pardot. All are point and click options, so automating Pardot is straight forward conceptually and no coding experience is required.

**Page Actions:** This feature specifically increases or decreases an individual's Lead Score based on a webpage they visited on your company's website or tracked page. Page Actions only requires a name for the Page Action you would like to create, the Page URL and input the Page Score as a negative or positive number to increase or decrease the Prospect's score. An example on how to utilize this feature is when a Prospect visits your website a number of times, but the page that is mainly being visited is your company career page. In this case, you want to decrease their score as they may not actually be a true prospect (even if they completed forms to gain access to various content). On the contrary, if there are webpages on your website that are highly valuable, and if Prospects eventually get to a high valued page, then you may want to increment their Lead Score more than the standard website visit score that is set within your Lead Scoring model.

A few settings related to Page Actions are the following:
- **'Priority Page?'** – If this setting is check marked for a Page Action URL, then this activity will be specifically shown as a Page Action item that is clearly visible to your internal Pardot and Salesforce CRM users as a high value or low value webpage visit as its own marketing activity record that is logged for all to view.
- **Completion Actions** – Just like on Form submissions as described earlier in this book, you can add various actions for the prospect to be subscribed to a specific list, create a task to a Salesforce CRM user, update a field and many other actions for each specific Page Action that you create.

**Helpful Hint:** This feature is used mostly for companies that have a well-developed website that has multiple tabs and pages, since Page Actions are based on specific webpage URL's.

**Automation Rules:** This feature automates a process based on rules that have specific criteria that filters records that match those rules, to then take a specific action(s). In simplistic terms, Automation Rules are 'If, Then' statements and are created by point-and-click options, not code.

There are three parts to an Automation Rule:
- **Part 1** - Name the rule, place it in a folder, add a description, add tags (if necessary) and determine if this is a 'Repeat Rule', meaning that prospects can go through this Automation Rule more than once.
- **Part 2** – Add your Rules that have criteria of what specific Prospect records you would like to include in this Automation Rule. You have the choice to select 'Match all', which are 'And' items that requires all criteria to match or you can choose 'Match any', which are 'Or' items that simply have to match part of the specific criteria inputted. Lastly you can add one-off Rules by clicking on the 'Add new rule' button, or you can add groups of rules combined within a set of rules by clicking on the 'Add new rule group' button. When you add a new rule group, you can either select "Match any' or 'Match all' within the rule group. This is in addition to the 'Match any' or 'Match all' that was set initially for the overall Rule. Examples of rules that can be created include if a Prospect was part of a specific campaign, and/or if they opened a specific email, and/or has a specific lead score, and/or has a field populated with a specific designation, etc. These are just a few items that can determine which Prospects to include within each automation that matched the inputted criteria.
- **Part 3** – Add your Actions of what happens to these records that matched the rule(s) for the specific Automation Rule that was created. Would you like to add them to a specific list, update a field, sync into Salesforce CRM, increase their Lead Score, add a Tag to their prospect record, add to a specific campaign or something else? Remember, there could be multiple Actions added that can take place within a single Automation Rule and it is important to review what you are trying to accomplish per Automation Rule to ensure the automation achieves your objective.

**Helpful Hint:** This feature is simple to use, but it is up to you to create the criteria and the logic behind what happens, providing nearly unlimited possibilities of what you would like to automate within Pardot. You will have to think through various scenarios of how each Automation Rule could impact your Prospects, processes and to not potentially overlap or conflict with other Automation Rules or processes that may cause redundancies or errors.

**Engagement Studio:** This is the last automation that is discussed within this book, as it is one of the main features of marketing automation. Engagement Studio allows you to create campaigns that utilize various assets (lists, emails, landing pages, forms) within a campaign canvas that displays each step of the automated campaign. Engagement Studio can be used for 'Nurture' or 'Drips' campaigns, automated campaigns for webinar/event/tradeshow registrations and targeted campaigns that have a specific focus over a period of time. Remember, the Engagement Studio is like a canvas in which you drag and drop Assets that you would like to use within the Campaign and create decisions and actions for the Prospects to follow various journey paths that are built within the canvas. Based on the Prospect's actions or lack thereof, will then determine if they receive the next set of email assets/communications and/or other actions that you want to happen.

A general example of utilizing the Engagement Studio is the following: the chosen targeted segment receives email #1 and a 'wait' step is added to wait for 3 days. Then a decision rule is placed to determine if anyone from the targeted segment has submitted the Form that was built for this specific Campaign. The recipients that did not submit the Form successfully, are then sent email #2 and repeats the same wait step, but this time it waits for 7 days with the decision rule to determine if anyone who received email #2 submitted the Form. Any recipient that did submit the Form successfully is then removed from the Campaign as they completed your Campaign objective in completing the designated Form, and were set to sync into Salesforce CRM and created a follow up task for sales to contact the Prospect accordingly. This can go on for as long as you want and will differ depending on the goal of each Campaign that you build. All of this logic and strategic timing of who and when each Prospect receives each type of communication, are all built by clicks (not code) and is displayed within a canvas format that clearly shows each step that you build within Engagement Studio.

# Step 9: Integrating Pardot with Salesforce & Other Connectors

NOW THAT YOUR PARDOT HAS nearly all the main features implemented and is working accordingly, it is ideal to integrate both Pardot and Salesforce CRM. This is necessary to do if you are wanting to have optimal reporting capabilities of marketing initiatives on a per campaign basis. If you have never activated the connector after installing the Pardot AppExchange Package, then the status of the connector will be defaulted to the 'Pause' status, which is ideal while you are setting up Pardot. There are settings within this connector that need to be reviewed prior to activating the Pardot sync. One of the most important settings is to ensure the 'Salesforce User Sync' is setup correctly to have the ability to manage Pardot users and auto-sync users from within Salesforce CRM into Pardot. Again, all of the settings within the Salesforce/Pardot sync are simple and there are not that many of them. Be sure to review each individual setting in full, to either enable or disable what is appropriate for your company's needs. Lastly, it is recommended that the designated "Connected User" for the Salesforce/Pardot Connector is the free license user that is provided by Salesforce called 'b2bmainintegration'. This way, you can track updates from Pardot into Salesforce by having this standard Salesforce/Pardot integration user be the designated 'Created By' or 'Last Modified By' user, that creates or updates various records from Pardot into Salesforce.

Connectors are available to integrate Pardot with a number of other items such as Social Media Platforms, Webinar programs, AdWords, and many others. This is a great way to truly centralize a variety of marketing initiatives and to see how they perform within a single platform.

# Step 10: Campaign Performance

FINALLY, THE MOMENT YOU HAVE have been waiting for has arrived! Now that you know about the majority of the main features that Pardot has to offer and you have implemented them accordingly, it is time to experience the benefits of having Pardot and Salesforce CRM working as a single unit and tracking or automating various items for optimal campaign reporting.

Before we dive right in, let's pause for a moment to discuss what is a Campaign 'success' and 'failure'. This is something that no one really talks about, but is one of the most important aspects of marketing automation. The truth is, every Campaign has a different goal. These goals must be established prior to activating any marketing Campaign. For example, is the goal of a specific Campaign to generate new Leads? Or is the goal to generate a certain response rate or a specific revenue benchmark? Even the most experienced marketers tend to forget to set Campaign goals on a per campaign basis, and their determination of a 'success or 'failure' may be different than what everyone else thought, because of differing Campaign goals. For example, is a Campaign successful if it delivered one thousand leads, but only one sales opportunity closed successfully generating $5,000.00? Or is a Campaign successful if it delivered only two Leads, had a 100% conversion rate and closed $200,000.00 in revenue? Always set clear Campaign goals and define the purpose of each Campaign prior to executing the actual Campaign. This sets the precedence with your team, other departments and executives, when reviewing various Campaign performance reports, in deeming them as 'successes' or 'failures'.

When Campaigns are built in Pardot, be sure to also create a corresponding Campaign record within Salesforce on the Campaign Object. Be sure to have the Campaign record that was created in Salesforce actually 'connected' to the Campaign record within Pardot. This will allow each Asset and Pardot tracked items, to be passed through and shown in the Campaign record within Salesforce. In summary, by connecting each Campaign created in Pardot to a Salesforce Campaign record, it shows a full picture of overall Campaign performance.

Within the Campaign record created in Salesforce, it also shows how many

Leads were associated to the Campaign, how many were converted and how many Contacts were associated to the Campaign, based on Completion Actions and/or the use of Automation Rules. These Prospects associated to each Campaign are known as "Campaign Member" records within Salesforce. Each Campaign Member will have a status and the system defaults are 'Sent' and 'Responded', but these can be set to whatever you choose as options on a per Campaign basis. An example of how these statuses can be used and updated is the following: 'Sent' status is that the Prospect was part of the Campaign and if the Prospect completes the Campaign Form, then one of the Completion Actions for that Form can be to update the Campaign Member Status to 'Responded', to calculate the overall Campaign Response Rate.

ROI (Return on Investment) calculations on a per Campaign basis can be accomplished by users relating an Opportunity to a specific campaign record to attribute the amount of pipeline and revenue generated per Campaign. If users create Opportunities at the Contact Object level, then the Opportunity will automatically associate the most recent Campaign record related to the Contact as the 'Primary Campaign Source' to attribute pipeline and revenue (if the Opportunity was won) to the Campaign record.

**Helpful Hint:** It is best to create Opportunities at the Contact level or associate 'Contact Roles' after creating an Opportunity, as this information will be synced back into Pardot to show which 'Prospects' have Opportunities linked to their profiles. This Opportunity history may affect their Lead Score and could include or exclude them from various campaigns due to List Rules, Automation Rules, etc., as this is a key part of having complete 'Prospect' profiles and attributing revenue to Campaigns within Pardot. This process automatically happens if a Salesforce user converts a Lead record.

And now, we finally come down to the reports and the true reason as to why you went through all this effort to implement various Pardot features, sync with Salesforce and have connected Campaigns to track Campaign Member associations from Leads/Contacts to Opportunity pipeline/revenue per Campaign.

Your reports could include the following that can be created within Salesforce CRM:
- **Marketing Only Delivered Leads:** This is now easy to track due to the Pardot integration user being set as the 'b2bmainintegration' user and therefore, any Leads created by this user are Leads that marketing delivered to sales.
- **Leads Delivered Overall:** Regardless if Leads were created by Marketing

or existed prior, you can report on the Campaign Object based on Leads and the Leads Converted fields for the total counts of Leads per Campaign. One example that allows you to report on specific Lead details is by creating a 'Campaign with Leads' report (you must choose a 'with Leads' or 'with Converted Leads' report type) to include the Lead Status field and other information to determine the quality of Leads delivered. This is just one example, as there are a number of ways to report on each Campaign Member's status per Campaign that may require additional customizations to be implemented.

- **Lead Conversion % per Campaign:** One way is to create a formula field that takes the Leads Converted field and divides by the number of Leads plus Leads Converted fields added together from the Campaign Object. This new formula field can be used within a Campaign Report.
- **Number of existing Contacts that re-engaged:** Reference the number of Contacts on the Campaign record less the number of Converted Leads field to calculate re-engagement efforts of existing Contacts.
- **Pipeline Generated:** Reference the fields called 'Opportunities in Campaign' and 'Value Opportunities in Campaign' on the Campaign record to get Pipeline information. A 'Campaigns with Opportunities' report can be utilized to get detailed level information regarding each Opportunity, products/services associated to each Opportunity, Stage etc.
- **Revenue Generated:** Reference the fields called 'Won Opportunities in Campaign' and 'Value Won Opportunities in Campaign' for calculations of ROI per campaign on the Campaign Record. You can also pull a 'Campaigns with Opportunities' report to get specific Opportunity details.
- **Lost Revenue:** 'Campaigns with Opportunities' report to get detailed level information regarding each Opportunity that was set to Closed Lost. It is recommended to have a Closed Lost Reason field to conclude why Opportunities are being lost.

**Helpful Hint:** There is a standard field called 'Type' on the Campaign Object and this should be customized to the types of Campaign classifications your company and marketing department will be executing. Therefore, each Campaign can be grouped by 'Type' to see which of the designated Campaign Types are overall the best performing and be able to drill down into each specific Campaign included within that Type that performed the best/worst. Reporting and grouping on this Campaign 'Type' field will tell you fairly quickly the types of Campaigns that perform the best/worst (based on whatever the Campaign goals are) that is determined by actual data-driven analytics from having Salesforce/Pardot working together to achieve 'Closed Loop Reporting'.

- **For Pardot Asset Performance** – Pardot is ideal to review which emails had the highest open/click thru rates, along with Landing Page analysis and Forms with the highest conversion rates. These should be reviewed while Campaigns are running to see if adjustments need to be made to improve performance and to review at designated times after Campaigns are completed, to continue to build on what was successful and update items that failed to meet expectations.

There you have it! Optimal Campaign reporting for marketing to clearly demonstrate how their efforts are adding value in a number of ways and how each initiative makes an impact on the company overall. With the use of Pardot that is synced with Salesforce CRM, the sales team is extremely happy that marketing is re-engaging various Leads/Contacts and also thankful for the new Leads that are being generated on their behalf. Executives are now able to see reports that exemplify everyone's efforts to make data driven decisions to continue building the organization. And YOU! Let's just say you are about to make a significant impact on your organization by just reading this book, and are now ready to get started with optimizing Pardot!

# Step 11: Consulting Partner

IT IS IDEAL TO HIRE experts regarding Salesforce or Pardot customizations, that can implement the business requirements you and your team have now compiled or are looking to accomplish. Our recommended Consulting Partners that specialize in Salesforce Implementations, Salesforce Customizations, Salesforce Training, Salesforce Monthly Management and Pardot can be requested directly through our website on the Contact Us page.

Printed in Great Britain
by Amazon

19408655R00021